POLICE LAB

Using Science to Solve Crimes

by ROBERT SHEELY

LEO BAUTISTA
706 E. Nikote Creek Court
Smithville, N.J. 08205

SILVER MOON PRESS

The author would like to thank Sergeant Bill Hinz of the Minneapolis Police Department, Don Melander of the Minnesota Bureau of Criminal Apprehension, the FBI Public Relations Unit, and Vara Kamin for their help, advice, and support.

The publisher would like to thank Dr. Robert E. Gaensslen, Director of Forensic Sciences at the University of New Haven, and Ed Guzdek, President of the Police Conference of New York, for their assistance in reviewing this book.

PHOTOGRAPH CREDITS: Library of Congress: frontispiece, p. 14; UPI/Bettman: pp. 2, 12 bottom; Federal Bureau of Investigation: pp. 3, 4, 5, 17, 23 top and bottom, 24, 43; The New York Times/Vic DeLucia: pp. 6, 7; AP/Wide World Photos: pp. 11, 20; New York State Criminalistics Research Bureau: p. 12 top; Comstock Inc./Russ Kinne: pp. 13, 38; Illustrations from THE CENTURY OF THE DETECTIVE by Jürgen Thorwald, copyright © 1964 by Droemersche Verlagsanstalt A.G. Zurich, English translation copyright © 1965 by Jürgen Thorwald, reprinted by permission of Harcourt Brace & Company: pp. 30, 32.

For information contact:
Silver Moon Press
New York, NY
(800) 874-3320

Distributed to the trade by: **August House**
PO Box 3223, Little Rock, AR 72203
(800) 284-8784

Project Editor: *Louise E. May*
Designer: *Jan Foster*
Cover: *Geoffrey Notkin*

Printed in the United States of America

Library of Congress Cataloging in Publication Data
Sheely, Robert, 1956-
    Police lab: using science to solve crimes / by Robert Sheely.—1st ed.
    p. cm.
    Includes bibliographical references and index.
SUMMARY: Describes the importance of forensic science in solving crimes and illustrates through case histories the role of science in crime detection and investigation.
ISBN 1-881889-40-8 : $13.95
1. Forensic sciences—Juvenile literature. 2. Crime laboratories—Juvenile literature. [1. Forensic sciences. 2. Crime laboratories. 3. Criminal investigation.] I. Title.
HV8073.S425 1993   93-4543
363.2'56--dc20   CIP AC

1896 — System of using fingerprints to identify people was developed by Edward Henry of England.

Basic human blood groups were discovered by Karl Landsteiner of Austria. — **1901**

1903 — New York City police department began fingerprinting arrested persons.

World's first forensic science laboratory was set up in France by Edmond Locard. — **1910**

1911 — Fingerprints were first accepted as evidence in a United States court.

First polygraph machine was built by John Larson of the United States. — **1921**

1924 — J. Edgar Hoover became head of the United States Federal Bureau of Investigation (FBI) and built it into a modern crime-detection agency.

FBI national fingerprint file was established. — **1930**

1932 — FBI forensic science laboratory was set up.

FBI's National Crime Information Center (NCIC) was set up. — **1967**

1980 — Method of detecting differences in DNA was discovered by Ray White of the United States.

Patrol car personal computers were first used in the United States to record crime reports and obtain immediate information from the NCIC. — **1983**

1987 — DNA test was first used as evidence in the United States to convict a person of a crime.

Notebook-sized computer for recording fingerprints and taking mug shots at a crime scene was developed in the United States. — **1993**

Contents

Chapter 1

Detectives in Lab Coats

A window is shattered. Broken glass covers the floor. Furniture is broken and valuable items are missing. A family arrives home to the shocking mess. As the parents wander through the house, looking in silent disbelief at the damage, one of their children picks up the phone and calls the police.

A burglary has taken place. The family's home has been broken into and its privacy has been disturbed. An ordinary home has been turned into the scene of a crime.

The police soon arrive to help the family. Police officers talk to the neighbors to learn if anyone saw the crime take place. Detectives scour the scene, looking for evidence that might point to a suspect.

Far from where the crime took place, special

detectives are working in a police lab. These detectives are scientists, and they are waiting to examine the evidence gathered by the detectives at the crime scene.

Throughout this book you will find yourself at a number of actual crime scenes from history and from today's police files. You will meet criminals and the police officers who track them down. In addition, you will see how scientists work with

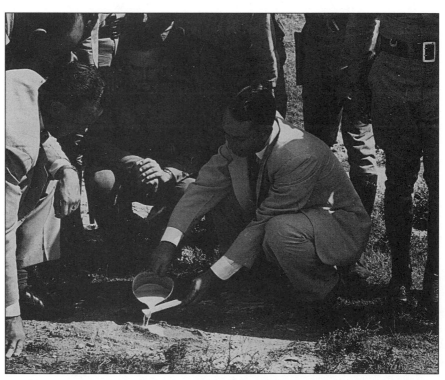

Making a plaster cast of a footprint left on the ground at the scene of a crime. Comparing a suspect's shoes to a cast can link the suspect to the crime.

Detectives in Lab Coats

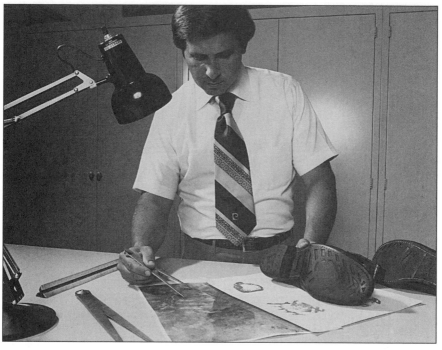

Footprints may also be photographed at a crime scene. The expert here is comparing the photo of a footprint with a suspect's shoes.

the police. You will learn about forensic science, the science that examines and studies evidence in order to solve crimes and convict criminals.

Police work and scientific research have a lot in common. In both, a person examines a mystery and gathers information about it. For a scientific researcher, the mystery to be solved may be an unexpected result in an experiment. For a police detective, the mystery to be solved is a crime. Once evidence about the mystery has been gathered, the next step for the researcher or detective is to form a hypothesis.

Detectives in Lab Coats

Searching some of the many reference files kept by the FBI Laboratory for information that will help identify and interpret evidence.

A hypothesis is a theory based on facts that is used to explain evidence. In the case of a detective, the hypothesis usually involves a suspect, a person the detective believes is guilty of the crime. And finally, both researchers and detectives must seek more information either to prove or disprove a hypothesis. For the detective, the goal is to find enough evidence to prove the suspect is guilty.

In forensic science, the tools of science are used to solve crimes. Evidence is gathered at the scene of a crime. Then the evidence is taken to a police laboratory for examination. Footprints, fingerprints, fibers, hair, handwriting, gunpowder, weapons, and bloodstains are some of the many types of evidence that

Detectives in Lab Coats

may be left behind at the scene of a crime. Body cells, which contain special particles called DNA, bite marks, and voiceprints may also be used as evidence. It is the job of the police lab to interpret all this evidence and provide the detectives with the information they need to identify a suspect.

Forensic scientists are always trying to improve the ways in which they use science to solve crimes. At the Forensic Science Research and Training Center in Quantico, Virginia, new methods of examining, studying, and interpreting evidence are developed and tested. The Center also trains officers, detectives, and police lab scientists from all across the country to use these new methods when they are trying to solve crimes.

State and local crime lab scientists receiving hands-on training in the latest methods of examining evidence at the Forensic Science Research and Training Center in Quantico, Virginia.

Once detectives have evidence and a suspect, the next step is a trial. At a trial, a detective's hypothesis is shown to be true or false. Under the legal system in the United States, a person is innocent until proven guilty. The trial is where the person is found to be guilty or not guilty. A lawyer working for the government, called a prosecutor, presents the evidence gathered by the police. The prosecutor also calls witnesses, people who have some information about the crime. Using the evidence along with the stories told by the witnesses, the prosecutor tries to prove that the suspect did indeed commit the crime.

VIC DeLUCIA

Measuring a bullet found at the scene of a crime. The bullet will also be weighed, checked for marks left by the gun barrel, and examined under a microscope. The bullet may also be compared with photographs of bullets from a reference file.

After the prosecutor presents his or her case, the lawyer for the suspect has a chance to present the suspect's side of the story. When both sides have presented their cases, a judge or jury decides if the suspect is guilty or not guilty.

Forensic science is an important tool for solving crimes. Without it, the

Detectives in Lab Coats

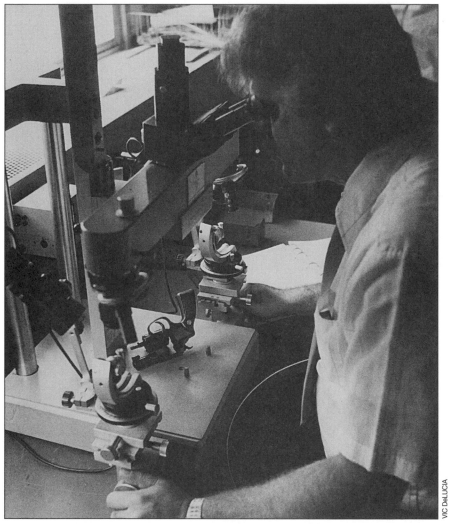

Firearms expert examining a gun under a microscope. When a gun is received at a police lab, the first step is to identify it and check it for fingerprints and unusual marks.

police would find it almost impossible to win trials and send criminals to jail. At the same time, forensic science helps the suspects in criminal cases. The scientific investigation of evidence can often prove that

7

an apparently guilty person is actually innocent. In the end, forensic science is like all science. It searches for the truth.

NOTE: The stories in this book are dramatizations of actual cases from police files past and present. Some details, such as names, have been changed. Many of the quotations have been made up to give the reader a sense of really being at the scene of the crime. However, the author has done his best to make sure the cases are real and the scientific principles are true and accurate.

Pointing a Finger

NEW YORK CITY, 1911. "We went to a show that night," the woman said, her voice steady. "Then we went home and to bed. My husband never left the house until the next morning. So there's no way he could have committed that burglary."

The woman peered out from the witness stand. Her eyes met her husband's eyes. He smiled faintly and nodded once, sitting quietly in the courtroom while his wife testified. His name was Caesar Cella. He was a notorious thief with a long record of burglaries in New York City.

On the night Mrs. Cella described, a shop in the heart of the city had been broken into. Unfortunately for the police, there were no eyewitnesses to the burglary. In fact, the only people to testify were five witnesses who swore they had been with Cella and his wife at the show that night.

"Are you absolutely certain, ma'am?" the prosecutor asked Mrs. Cella. As he had done with each of the other witnesses, the prosecutor tried his best to get her to change her story. But it was no use. She stuck by everything she had said. One look at the judge's grim face and the prosecutor knew he was losing the case. Unless he could present some solid evidence that Cella had been at the scene of the crime, Cella would go free.

The prosecutor had one last chance to win the case. He decided to take it.

"Your honor," he said, "I call Detective Sergeant Joseph A. Faurot to the stand."

Every eye in the courtroom was on the young detective as he came forward. Sergeant Faurot took the stand and calmly answered the prosecutor's questions in a strong, clear voice.

"Did you examine the scene of the crime, Sergeant Faurot?" asked the prosecutor.

"Yes," replied Sergeant Faurot.

"Did you discover anything important?"

"I found some marks on a window frame."

"What kind of marks?"

"The prints of several dirty fingers."

"And why are these prints important?"

"I have been studying a new method that allows me to identify a person by his or her fingerprints," replied Faurot. "In fact, over the last few years I have collected samples of the fingerprints of a number of criminals."

Pointing a Finger

Detective looking for fingerprints on a window at the scene of a homicide. When prints are found, they are photographed and then removed with tape.

"Were you able to match the prints from the window frame to any of your samples?"

"Yes, I was," said Faurot, turning to the jury. "The fingerprints at the crime scene are those of the defendant, Caesar Cella!"

Noisy confusion broke out in the courtroom. No one had ever heard of these "fingerprints" before. The judge banged his gavel and shouted, "Order!" Finally the people settled back into their seats, eager to see what would happen next. Would the judge accept this new evidence? Would a few dirty marks on a window frame be enough to convict Caesar Cella? Or would he go free?

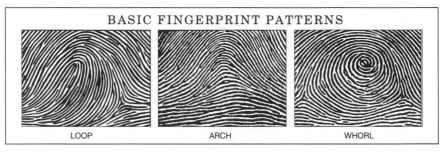

BASIC FINGERPRINT PATTERNS

LOOP   ARCH   WHORL

The three basic fingerprint patterns. The basic patterns are further broken down into groups by characteristics such as the number of ridges between two points, ridge branches, and islands.

Everyone who has ever read a mystery story or watched a police show on TV has heard about fingerprints. But what exactly are they? Look closely at the tips of your fingers. You will see each finger is covered with tiny ridges. These ridges make a pattern that never changes. When you touch something, oils from your skin leave a print of this pattern on the surface you touch. The pattern is your fingerprint.

But why do your fingers have ridges in the first place? The answer is simple. The ridges help you grasp and hold onto things. They act like the stick-ons some people put on

Fingerprints on a glass jar. Fingerprints are an important source of evidence for identifying suspects.

Pointing a Finger

Fingerprinting an arrested suspect. In most cities in the United States, every person arrested is fingerprinted.

the bottom of the bathtub to keep their feet from slipping. The ridges on your fingers, and also on the palms of your hands, keep things from slipping out of your hands.

Scientists divide fingerprints into different categories according to the patterns made by the ridges. The three basic patterns are loops, whorls, and arches. The amazing thing is, no two fingerprints are exactly alike. Each person's fingerprints are different from everyone else's. This is why fingerprints can be used to identify people.

Most of the fingerprints we leave behind are invisible to the naked eye. You really cannot see your fingerprints unless you touch something with dirty

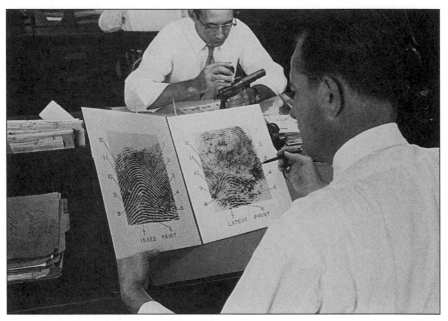

Comparing a fingerprint from a suspect (inked print) to a print found at the scene of a crime (latent print). When comparing fingerprints, it takes ten or more identical points to declare the prints a match.

hands. But this does not mean criminals must have dirty hands before the police can find their fingerprints. To find the invisible fingerprints left by criminals, police detectives "dust" the scene of a crime. What they actually do is spread a thin layer of fine powder on the surface they want to test. The dusting powder sticks to the skin oils left behind by the criminal's fingers. When the detective brushes away the loose powder, the fingerprints become visible. The prints are then photographed and kept as evidence. The prints are also removed, or lifted, with clear tape and placed on a fingerprint card.

Dusting for fingerprints works best on smooth, hard surfaces like glass or metal. To find prints on other surfaces, such as paper and wood, detectives use chemicals that darken when they come into contact with the skin oils.

When a suspect is arrested, police take a complete set of her or his fingerprints. They roll the suspect's fingertips in ink and then press them onto a fingerprint card. This card is stored in police files. Later, when the police find fingerprints at a crime scene, they compare the new prints to the fingerprints they have on file. Today, many police departments store their fingerprint files on computers. This makes it possible for police departments to store millions of fingerprints and to share them with other departments across the nation.

Without fingerprints it would be very hard for the police to solve crimes. But it was not until the late 1800s that the police began to become interested in fingerprints. People had been aware of the ridges on their fingertips, but they had not thought of using them to solve crimes.

In the 1870s, William Herschel, a British official in India, began experimenting with fingerprints as a hobby. He collected prints from a number of people and studied them. After a while he realized that no two people's fingerprints were exactly alike. Herschel soon became excited about the possibility of using fingerprints as a way of identifying people.

Over the next 35 years, individual police officers such as Sergeant Faurot began to take notice of Herschel's discovery. They used fingerprinting in their own investigations. But there was no widespread system for fingerprinting criminals in the United States. By 1911, one important question still waited to be answered. Would fingerprints be accepted as evidence in a criminal trial?

After the people in the courtroom returned to order, Caesar Cella's lawyer rose from his chair and prepared to cross-examine Sergeant Faurot.

"Do you honestly expect us to trust these finger smudges over the sworn testimony of five people?" he asked. "Because either they are all liars or your little fingerprints are nothing more than pure bunk."

How was the jury to decide? This was the first time a court in the United States was being asked to convict a person solely on the evidence of fingerprints. No one wanted to risk sending an innocent person to jail. But Sergeant Faurot's testimony had been very convincing.

Finally the judge came up with an idea. He had Sergeant Faurot leave the courtroom. Then the judge asked fifteen people from the courtroom to press their right index fingers against the glass of the windows. One of the fifteen people was also asked to press the same finger against the glass on the top of the judge's desk.

Complete set of fingerprints for John Dillinger, one of the most famous criminals in United States history. After these prints were taken, Dillinger escaped from jail and tried to have his fingerprints removed from his fingertips.

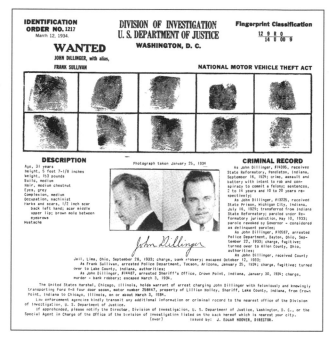

The judge then sent for Faurot and asked him to identify which print on the windows matched the one on his glass desktop. Faurot took out a large magnifying glass and went to work studying the prints. Within four minutes he identified the correct print. The jury stared at Faurot, their mouths hanging open in awe. Some people in the courtroom actually started to clap.

Faced with this proof of the power of fingerprints, Cella admitted everything. He said he had indeed gone to the show that night, and then to bed. But after his wife fell asleep, he sneaked out of the house and broke into the shop. He then returned home and to bed without even waking her.

17

This case was an historic event. For the first time, a United States court had accepted fingerprints as evidence in a criminal trial. In the years that followed, many other criminals found themselves in Caesar Cella's shoes. They were convicted on the evidence of their own fingertips.

Chapter 3

The Fatal Fiber

MINNEAPOLIS, MINNESOTA, 1986. It was six o'clock in the morning. Everything was quiet at the TV station. Suddenly the quiet was shattered by the loud ringing of a telephone in the empty news department. A security guard who happened to be passing by stepped into the room and picked up the phone.

"Hello," the guard said.

"Is this WZZZ?" asked the caller.

"Yes."

"I just saw a murder."

"What?" The guard gripped the phone tightly.

"I saw a murder," the caller said. "Go to the parking lot on the corner of 24th and Lindsay Streets and you'll find a body."

"Who is this?" demanded the security guard. But it was too late. The caller had already hung up.

A news crew went immediately to the parking

The Fatal Fiber

Police officer examining a body at a murder scene. After the scene is photographed and the body removed, each piece of evidence collected by the police will be sent to a crime lab for examination. The body will also be examined to determine the exact cause of death and for additional evidence.

lot named by the caller. In the early morning light the crew members could see a couple of truck trailers parked next to a building. Under one of the trailers was a dark shape.

The crew members glanced quickly at each other. Then they took a few steps toward the trailer. They saw that the shape was a body.

A dead body.

Using the radio in the news van, one of the crew called the police. Within minutes a squad car pulled up. Officers Bob Nestor and Denise Thompson hopped out and strode over to the news van.

"Okay," said Thompson. "What do you have?"

"Over here," said the camera operator, leading the officers over to the trailer.

When the officers bent down to look at the body underneath, they found one of the strangest sights they had ever seen.

"She's green!" exclaimed Officer Nestor.

Indeed, the dead woman's skin and long hair were streaked with bright green paint. The officers looked at each other and shook their heads. They had seen many grisly and unusual things over the years, but nothing quite like this Green Lady.

Nestor and Thompson sealed off the crime scene. Then they waited for the homicide detectives to arrive. Homicide is another word for murder, and homicide detectives investigate murders. When the homicide detectives arrived, they carefully examined the scene. Then they called in the Bureau of Identification.

The Bureau of Identification is the department within the Minneapolis Police Force that collects and studies physical evidence. Physical evidence provides most of the clues the police use to solve crimes. It includes anything left by a criminal at the scene of a crime, such as threads, fingerprints, wire, hair, fibers, weapons, footprints, or tire tracks.

In the case of the Green Lady, Bureau of Identification officers found several pieces of physical evidence. They collected all of them because they had no way of knowing which would be important and which would not. Then one of the officers knelt down a few feet from the body.

"Look at this," the officer said.

"What is it?" asked another officer.

"Some kind of fiber."

The first officer pointed to a small green fiber lying on the ground. What neither officer knew at the time was that this tiny clue, barely an inch long and less than a quarter-inch thick, was all it would take to crack the case and bring the Green Lady's killer to justice.

Physical evidence is analyzed, or studied, in a forensic lab. There, for example, a fiber from a crime scene can be compared with a fiber from the clothes of a suspect. Two special instruments, a comparison microscope and a polarized light microscope, are used to compare fibers.

A microscope magnifies an object many times its original size and shows details that cannot be seen by the naked eye. A comparison microscope actually contains two microscopes. A lab scientist places a sample fiber under each microscope. The samples are magnified as much as 400 times their original size and then shown side-by-side on a video monitor screen. The fibers are also examined under a polarized light microscope. This microscope eliminates the effects of dyes so the true characteristics of the fibers can be discovered.

Finally, lab scientists compare the magnified

Removing part of a bloodstain from clothing. The stain will be examined under a microscope and tested with chemicals to see if it is human blood. If it is, the blood will be further tested to determine its type.

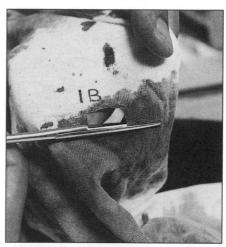

Magnified view of a paint chip from the door of a house that was broken into. Twenty-two different colored layers of paint are visible.

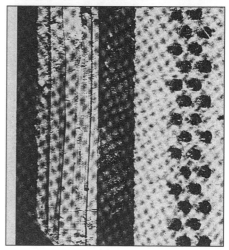

samples. They look to see if the fibers are made from the same materials, such as cotton, wool, nylon, rayon, or polyester. They also study the characteristics of the fibers and examine details such as the thicknesses and shapes of the fibers.

Paint samples are another type of physical evidence. They can be placed under a powerful microscope and magnified hundreds of times their original

The Fatal Fiber

Analyzing a chemical substance in a computerized gas chromato-graph. Drugs, explosives, gasoline, paint, ink, and alcohol are some of the substances that can be identified with this instrument.

size. Lab scientists then compare the colors along with the gloss, or shininess, of the paint samples. If the two samples appear to be the same, further tests can be performed.

One of these tests is called a solubility test. Tiny chips are scraped off each paint sample. Then the chips are dipped into different chemicals. Scientists study how the paint chips react to the chemicals. If the chips from both samples react the same way, the results may be considered as evidence the paint samples are from the same source.

An even more exact test of physical evidence uses a process called chromatography. Chromatography separates out the things that make up a mixture. The kind of chromatography used to test physical evidence is gas chromatography. In a gas chromatography test, a tiny sample of the substance to be tested is put inside a small glass tube. The glass tube is heated to over 700 degrees Fahrenheit. This high heat turns the sample into a gas. The different parts of the gas then flow at different speeds through a narrow, coiled tube. At the end of the tube is an electric detector connected to an ink pen. As electricity passes through the gas, it moves the ink pen, which makes a pattern on a moving strip of paper. If two different samples produce similar patterns, the samples may be from the same source.

With these and other tests, the forensic lab scientists compare evidence found at the scene of a crime with evidence found on a suspect or things belonging to the suspect. In the case of the Green Lady, the police had plenty of evidence. Now all they needed was a suspect.

A series of helpful breaks led the detectives quickly to the killer. The first break came when a truck driver approached the officers at the crime scene.

"Listen," the driver said. "I saw a car pull into this lot about five-thirty this morning. I thought it was kind of suspicious so I wrote down a description of the car."

The police soon found a car matching the truck driver's description. It was just a few blocks away in a gravel parking lot behind a run-down apartment building. The police approached the battered car carefully.

Then came the second break.

"Look!" exclaimed one of the officers, kneeling down to look at the ground. There, just a few feet from the car, was a green fiber that looked exactly like the one found at the scene of the crime.

A few feet further on, the officers found another green fiber. Then another, and yet another.

The trail of fibers led to a set of wooden stairs leading up the back of the apartment building. At the top of the stairs was a door. The detectives knocked on the door.

"Who is it?" a man asked nervously.

"Police. May we come in?"

The man opened the door. He was tall and thin. His eyes were red and bleary, and he looked like he hadn't slept all night.

The first thing the detectives noticed when they stepped inside was the carpet on the living room floor. It was a green shag carpet and it was the same shade of green as the green fiber found near the body. The carpet was old and rotten. It was easy to see how fibers could come loose from it.

The third break came while one detective was talking to the man in the living room. In the kitchen, another detective noticed a stain on the linoleum floor. The detective bent down to take a closer look. The stain was some kind of green paint.

Based on the green carpet fibers and the green paint stain, the detectives took the man down to the police station for questioning. At first the suspect denied knowing anything about the murder. But soon he broke down in tears and confessed.

"We had a fight," he told the detectives. "I lost my temper and started choking her. Then when I let go, she was still." When he realized what he had done, the man decided to try to cover up his crime.

"I thought I could make it look like some street gang killed her," the man said. In desperation he had grabbed a can of spray paint and painted the body. Then he carried the body out to his car and dropped it off in the parking lot. After that, he phoned the TV station.

The Bureau of Identification collected several pieces of evidence from the man's apartment, including fibers from the carpet. In the kitchen they found the can of green spray paint.

When this evidence was presented in court, the man was convicted of first-degree murder and given a life sentence in prison. The strange case of the Green Lady was solved.

Find That Poison

LE GLANDIER, FRANCE, 1840. The sky was dark. A cold rain pelted the bleak countryside. In a big, shadowy house a man lay in bed, terribly sick. He had all the symptoms of cholera, a terrible disease that could kill a person because it caused severe cramps, vomiting, and diarrhea.

As the winds howled outside, the man, whose name was Charles Lafarge, shivered and moaned. His pretty young wife Marie knelt by his side and handed him a glass.

"Here, darling," she whispered. "Drink this."

"What is it?" he gasped.

"Eggnog. Just like I've been giving you for weeks now."

With a trembling hand, Charles raised the glass to his lips and drank. Because he was so sick, Charles did not notice the white powder floating on the top of the eggnog. Nor did he notice the cold look in Marie's dark eyes.

A few short hours later Charles Lafarge was dead.

With no show of emotion at all, Marie went to her bedroom. There she dressed herself in black mourning clothes and prepared to visit her lawyer to learn about her husband's will. It was no secret she had married Charles for his money. Now, Marie thought, the money would all be hers.

Meanwhile, in another part of the house, a storm was brewing. And it was every bit as violent as the storm outside.

Charles's mother and sisters, along with several of the servants, stood in the hallway outside the dead man's room. Facing them was a distinguished man in a long black coat. His name was Dr. Lespinasse.

"Madame," he addressed the grieving mother, "I regret to say I have some disturbing news. After examining your son, I am quite certain he did not die of cholera."

"What do you mean?" the old lady gasped.

"Your son was poisoned with arsenic," the doctor replied.

Then Dr. Lespinasse explained. Arsenic is a white powder commonly used to poison rats. If a person swallows arsenic it produces cramps, vomiting, and a slow, painful death. The symptoms could easily be mistaken for cholera.

Marie Lafarge, who became famous for killing her husband by poisoning him with arsenic. The Lafarge trial focused world-wide interest on the new science of toxicology.

At this, several of the servants spoke up about the mysterious white powder they had seen Marie Lafarge mix into her husband's food.

"She sent me to town for arsenic only last week," said Alfred, the gardener. "She said it was for the rats."

Dr. Lespinasse knew in his own mind that Charles Lafarge had been poisoned. But proving he had been poisoned was a very different matter.

The police came and collected all the evidence they could find, including the glass of eggnog and even the dead man's body.

"Why are you taking my son?" wailed Lafarge's mother.

"If we are to find the truth," said the police officer, "we must get the answers to some questions. Questions only this dead man can answer."

Both the police and scientists had long dreamed of finding a test for poison. For centuries, poison was a silent killer because it was usually impossible to detect poison. While the police often suspected poison had been used, they were rarely able to prove it. Unless they had a confession or an eyewitness, the police had very little evidence to support a case for poisoning.

By the 1800s, rapid advances were taking place in the young science of toxicology, the science that studies poisons. In Paris, France, a scientist named Dr. Mathieu Orfila was hard at work trying to develop a test for the presence of arsenic. Orfila studied the chemical reactions that changed this tasteless, odorless poison that often became nearly invisible into something that could be seen. But he was not able to develop a test that made arsenic visible.

Meanwhile, an English scientist named James Marsh used information Dr. Orfila had discovered to develop an instrument to test for the presence of arsenic and make it visible. The instrument looked like a large jar with a stopper. Two glass tubes led out of the stopper. At the end of the longer tube was a

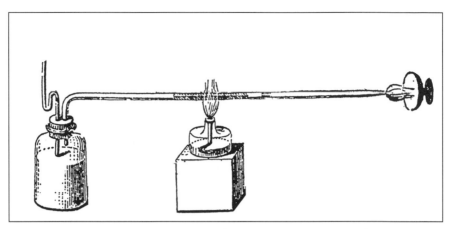

In 1836, James Marsh developed this instrument for the detection of arsenic. Today, a process called paper chromatography is one of the methods used to test for poisons.

nozzle and a small flame.

A sample of the substance to be tested was put into the jar. Then the chemicals sulfuric acid and zinc were added and a white dish was held in front of the flame. If there was arsenic in the sample, it would react with the sulfuric acid and zinc and turn into a gas called arsine. The arsine gas would then travel through the longer glass tube and escape from the nozzle. The flame in front of the nozzle would burn the arsine gas.

The dish in front of the flame was checked at the end of the test. If the dish was still clean, it meant the flame had not burned arsine gas and there was no arsenic in the sample. However, if there was a black deposit on the dish, it meant arsine gas had been burned and the sample contained arsenic. And the larger the black deposit, the more arsenic in the sample.

Almost anything suspected of containing arsenic could be tested using Marsh's instrument—even samples from the body of a dead person.

The trial of Marie Lafarge was one of the first times the new science of toxicology was put to use in a criminal case. Two separate groups of investigators tested Charles Lefarge's remains for arsenic. When they made their separate reports to the court, one group said it had found arsenic in Lafarge's body. The other group said it could not find any arsenic in the body!

The trial soon became the talk of France. People in every corner of the nation followed each detail in their daily newspapers. "Hang her!" said half of France. "She's innocent!" said the other half.

Finally the court sent for the great expert himself, Dr. Orfila. When he arrived, he insisted both groups of investigators follow him into the lab as witnesses. Soon he stood in the middle of a circle of scientists and prepared to begin his tests.

Dr. Orfila was brought the glass of eggnog that Marie Lafarge had made for her husband just before he died. Using Marsh's instrument, the test for arsenic was soon done.

"My word," exclaimed Orfila, "there's enough arsenic in this glass to kill ten people!"

But Dr. Orfila was not finished. The most important test lay ahead. He had to determine if there was arsenic in Lafarge's body.

Dr. Orfila took a small sample of the victim's stomach and put it in the testing tube. Then he added the sulfuric acid and zinc. As he worked, he explained to the scientists around him, "This next step is the most delicate part. The flame must be set just right. If it is too hot, it will drive off the gas." While he could not be certain, Orfila suspected using a too-hot flame was the mistake the earlier investigators had made.

Orfila adjusted the flame and began the test. The entire lab was silent. Every eye stared at the white dish. Then, slowly, above the flame there appeared a dark deposit.

"Arsenic," said Dr. Orfila. The rest of the scientists had no choice but to agree.

Dr. Orfila reported his results to the court and Marie Lafarge was sentenced to spend the rest of her life in prison. That gave her a lot of time to think about how she had been convicted by the most unlikely witness of all—her victim's body!

Chapter 5

Who Am I?

SAN FRANCISCO, CALIFORNIA, 1990. "Help me..." The soft, desperate voice came from just outside the sanctuary. *"Please, someone help me!"*

The pastor hurried out to the front hall of the church. There he found a tall, thin man with a dazed look in his eyes. Blood was running down his face.

"Oh, my!" exclaimed the pastor as he led the man to a nearby bench and helped him sit down. Taking out his handkerchief, the pastor wiped most of the blood from an ugly gash on the man's head. The man winced in pain.

"We need to get you to a hospital," said the pastor. "I'm Pastor Ben Smith. What's your name?"

"I—I don't know," said the man in a quiet, scared voice.

At the hospital emergency room a doctor examined the man's head. "How did this happen?" he asked.

"I remember walking along the sidewalk. I saw something out of the corner of my eye," said the man. "I turned and someone jumped out at me. Then everything went black. The next thing I remember, I was wandering around lost."

"That's when I found him," added Pastor Smith.

"What else do you remember?" asked the doctor.

"Not much," said the man. "Not my name or where I live or even if I have a family. What's the matter with me?"

"You appear to be suffering from amnesia," said the doctor.

"Amnesia?" repeated the man.

"Memory loss," explained the doctor. "It can be caused by a severe blow to the head such as the one you have suffered."

"Will I get my memory back?"

"It's hard to know. In some cases, a person's memory comes back over time. In other cases, it doesn't."

The man accepted this news in silence.

"His wallet is missing, too," said Pastor Smith. "The mugger must have taken it."

"So how do I find out who I am?" asked the Man Without a Name.

The next day a TV news crew came and interviewed the man. A reporter broadcast the story on the evening news and asked anyone who recognized the

man to come forward. But no one called the TV station. It looked like the man might never find out who he was.

Then a call came in from a person offering to help.

"Do you have information about who the Man Without a Name might be?" the caller was asked.

"No," the caller replied.

"Then how can you help?"

"I'm a special agent with the FBI."

The letters FBI stand for Federal Bureau of Investigation. The FBI is the closest thing the United States has to a national police force. In addition to investigating national crimes such as kidnappings and terrorism, the FBI offers assistance to state and local police forces. One of the main ways the FBI does this is by gathering information on crimes and criminals. It shares this information with other police forces through a computer system called the National Crime Information Center, or NCIC.

The NCIC is a huge computer network. It links the powerful FBI computers to computers in police departments across the country. Each individual police department's computers are connected to the NCIC computers by telephone lines. Just as people can talk to each other over telephone lines, so can computers "talk" to each other over these lines.

For example, a police officer in Dallas, Texas,

Officer in a police communications center checking with the NCIC for information about a crime. By 1989, the NCIC had records of over 20 million crimes stored in 12 different computer reference files.

can have a Dallas computer dial up an NCIC computer. Once connected, the Dallas computer can send the license plate number of a suspected stolen car. The information travels at high speed over a phone line to an NCIC computer. Once the information is there, the NCIC computer compares the license plate number to the millions of records of stolen cars it has in its memory.

If the Dallas license plate number matches any of the stolen cars listed in the NCIC computer, a message is sent back to the Dallas computer. The Dallas police can then seize the car and return it to its owner, even if the owner is thousands of miles away.

In addition to information on stolen cars, the

NCIC keeps records of many other things. It has records of stolen guns, stolen license plates, stolen stocks and bonds, stolen boats, wanted persons, missing persons, and unidentified persons such as the Man Without a Name.

In the case of the Man Without a Name, FBI Special Agent David Johnson saw the man's story on the TV news. He volunteered to help the man find out who he was. Johnson connected up with the NCIC computer network and entered the details of the unidentified man's description—his height, weight, hair color, eye color, and so on. Then Johnson waited for the computer to process the information. Within minutes, a message came back from the NCIC computer. The man's description matched up with a missing person report filed by the Nebraska State Patrol.

Special Agent Johnson took down the information and called the Nebraska State Patrol. He asked about the missing person report. He learned that a man named Rick Brown had left Nebraska on a trip to San Francisco. Special Agent Johnson double-checked the missing Mr. Brown's description. It matched the Man Without a Name perfectly.

Johnson drove to the hospital to tell the man the news.

"Your name is Rick Brown," Johnson said.

"Rick Brown?" said the man, trying to remember if the name sounded familiar.

"You're from Nebraska. You came here to San Francisco weeks ago on a bus. Your family…"

"I have a family?" asked the man.

"Yes," said Johnson, "and they were worried when they didn't hear from you. So they filed a missing person report, and that's what helped me find out who you are."

The man, no longer without a name, looked at Johnson with tears in his eyes. "Thank you," he said. "When that person mugged me, more than my wallet disappeared. My whole life disappeared. Now you have found it for me."

Special Agent Johnson smiled. "I'm just glad I could help you," he told Mr. Brown. "It's not always so easy to find out the true identity of an unidentified person."

A few days later, Rick Brown's family arrived at the hospital to take him home.

Looking for Liars

BUENA PARK, CALIFORNIA, 1967. It was a day just like any other at the First National Bank when a man stepped inside and looked around the lobby. He waited until there were only a few customers left in the bank. Then he walked up to a bank teller and pulled out a gun.

The teller's heart began to pound as the man pointed the gun at her and handed her a brown paper bag.

"Fill it up," he commanded.

Following the man's instructions, the teller emptied all the cash from her drawer into the bag. Her hands were shaking so badly she almost dropped some of the money. When she was done, the robber grabbed the bag from her and fled.

Later that day, when police detectives searched the crime scene, they weren't able to come up with any clues at first. Then finally they found one clue. It was on the teller's counter—a single fingerprint.

The fingerprint was dusted, lifted off the counter with clear tape, and placed in an evidence envelope. Back at the police station, the fingerprint from the evidence envelope was compared to the prints in the police files and a match was made. Based on this evidence, the police arrested a man named Brian Costanzo.

Costanzo denied having anything to do with the robbery. He told the police he owned a sandwich wagon. Every day he parked somewhere in the city and sold coffee and sandwiches. On the day of the robbery, he had parked his wagon more than eleven miles from the bank. Costanzo was even able to produce thirteen witnesses who swore they were buying food from him when the robbery was taking place.

In court, the case came down to the word of Costanzo and his thirteen witnesses against the single fingerprint. The jury believed the fingerprint. Brian Costanzo was sentenced to fifteen years in federal prison.

As the police led him away, Costanzo was filled with despair. He knew he was innocent. But how could he prove he was telling the truth?

For centuries, people searched for a way to determine the truthfulness of a person's words. In fact, many criminal trials came down to one person's word against another's. It had long been a dream of scientists to find a scientific method for figuring out when a person was telling the truth.

In 1921, Dr. John A. Larson built an instrument that became known as a polygraph. A polygraph takes four different measurements of a person's body and writes the results with moving pens on a long strip of paper.

The four things a polygraph measures are blood pressure, heartbeat, breathing rate, and rate of perspi-

Taking a polygraph test. The four wavy lines on the paper show the test taker's physical responses—heartbeat, blood pressure, breathing, perspiration—while answering a series of questions requiring yes or no answers.

ration. The principle behind the test is simple. When a person is in a situation that causes stress, his or her body changes slightly. Blood pressure rises, the heart beats faster, breathing speeds up, and more perspiration is produced.

A polygraph test works on the idea that when a person is questioned and lies, she or he is under stress. The changes in the body caused by this stress are recorded by the polygraph. So, to be absolutely correct, a polygraph does not detect lies. It measures the stress caused by lying.

It takes a skilled operator to give and interpret a polygraph test correctly. Experienced liars have fooled some operators. And operators who are not experienced sometimes mistake a person's nervousness about being questioned for lying. For these reasons, most courts do not accept polygraph test results as evidence. However, even if the results cannot be used in court, they can help point the way to the truth.

Brian Costanzo appealed his case and asked a higher court to throw out the guilty verdict. While the judge considered the case, he let Costanzo out on bail. Costanzo used this time to search for someone who believed him and would help him prove his innocence. Eventually he found his way to a private detective named Jim Moore. Moore offered to help Costanzo on one condition: Costanzo must take and pass a polygraph test.

Costanzo readily agreed. For almost four hours he answered questions. When he was done, the polygraph operator turned to Moore. "He's telling the truth," he said. "He didn't rob that bank."

Moore agreed to take Costanzo's case. But a few days later, Costanzo's lawyer called with bad news. The judge had denied Costanzo's appeal.

Costanzo was locked up in prison. Now Jim Moore was his only hope.

"Hang in there," said Moore. "I believe you and I'll do everything I can to get you out."

Moore got to work immediately. He interviewed witnesses, talked to the detectives who had investigated the robbery, and examined every piece of evidence. Soon Moore realized that the case came down to only one thing—the fingerprint on the bank counter.

Moore called a number of police officers who were his friends. He asked each one of them if they had ever known of a mistaken fingerprint. Over and over, the answer was no. Fingerprints do not lie. But finally one officer said, "Fingerprints don't lie, but fingerprint evidence can be faked."

With this hint, Moore went to the police authorities and asked to have the fingerprint evidence re-examined. And when the experts in the crime lab looked at the fingerprint under a powerful microscope, they noticed something very strange. The dusting powder on the fingerprint was not the kind used by the Buena Park police. In fact, the powder was the kind used in a photocopying machine.

No one may ever know for sure just what happened. The best guess is that someone in the police department took Brian Costanzo's fingerprint card from the police files and copied it on a photocopying machine. Then that person replaced the real fingerprint from the crime scene with the photocopy of Costanzo's fingerprint.

Maybe this person thought Costanzo was guilty and wanted to make sure he went to jail. Whatever the reason, an innocent man had been convicted of a crime.

Moore and the crime lab experts took their evidence back to the judge. The judge looked over the evidence and reversed the conviction.

Brian Costanzo was finally free to go.

Brian Costanzo's case is a fitting end to our look at forensic science. This case proves a very important point. Science is a useful tool for solving crimes, but it is not perfect. In the end, it is no more reliable than the people who use it.

Try These

Would you like to be a police lab detective? Here are some activities to get you started. You can do them at home by yourself or with a friend or an adult. Be sure to check with an adult before you begin any activity. And be sure to work carefully.

FINGERPRINTS

Making a Fingerprint Card
You can make a fingerprint card with your own fingerprints.

1. You will need a piece of paper, a pen or pencil, a ruler, and an inked stamp pad.
2. Write your name at the top of the paper. Then use the ruler to draw two rows of boxes with five boxes in each row. Label the top row *Right Hand* and the bottom row *Left Hand*. Then label the left box in each row *Thumb*. Label the next box in each row *Index*, the next box *Middle*, and the next box *Ring*. Label the last box in each row *Little*.
3. Start with your right hand. Roll your thumb on the ink pad. Then press your inked thumb inside the box labeled *Thumb* in the top row.

Name_____

RIGHT HAND

THUMB	INDEX	MIDDLE	RING	LITTLE

LEFT HAND

THUMB	INDEX	MIDDLE	RING	LITTLE

4. Repeat this process for your other nine fingers. Ink each finger and press it inside the correct box.
Now you have a set of your own fingerprints. If you would like to start a fingerprint file, ask your friends and family if you can make cards with their finger-prints.

Dusting and Lifting Fingerprints

You can lift fingerprints right from a piece of glass.

1. You will need talcum powder, clear tape, a sheet of glass or glass tabletop, a piece of black or dark paper, and a white or yellow crayon.

2. Ask a friend or family member to press his or her fingers on the glass.

3. Lightly sprinkle the powder on and around the prints. Then gently blow away any extra powder.

4. Press a piece of tape onto each print. Peel off the tape carefully so the fingerprint comes up with it.

5. Stick the pieces of tape onto the paper. Label the paper with the person's name.

If you have started a fingerprint file, you may want to lift the prints of several friends and family members and add them to your file.

SOLUBILITY

Comparing Reactions

You can see how different substances react to chemicals by doing this experiment.

1. You will need a small red cabbage, some red beets, a large knife, a stainless steel pot, a strainer, a mixing bowl, two large jars, a teaspoon, white vinegar, soap flakes (not detergent), cream of tartar, baking soda, paper, and a pen or pencil.

2. Chop up the cabbage and put it into the pot. Cover the cabbage with water.

3. Heat the cabbage and water on the stove until the water boils.

4. Collect the cabbage water, which should now be red, by pouring the contents of the pot through the strainer set over the mixing bowl. When the water cools, pour it into one of the jars until the jar is about half full. (You may want to have an adult help you with this step.)

5. Chop up the beets and follow steps 2-4 to make beet water.

6. Put both jars in the sink. Then stir about a teaspoon of white vinegar into each jar. Notice the changes in each jar and write down the results.

7. One-by-one, stir a teaspoon of soap flakes, cream of tartar, and baking soda into each jar. Notice the changes each time and record the results. (Eventually the water in each jar may foam up and overflow, so be careful when you add ingredients.)

Compare the results you got from the cabbage water and beet water. Did the waters react the same or differently? You can also make water from other red foods (strawberries, cherries, tomatoes) and red flowers and repeat the experiment. Then compare the new results to your cabbage and beet results.

CHROMATOGRAPHY

Identifying by Color Patterns

You can do a chromatography test and create color patterns of different felt-tip pens.

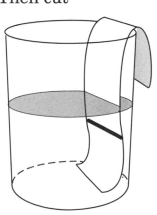

1. You will need a glass, paper towels, scissors, and several different brands of black felt-tip pens.
2. Fill the glass about half full of water. Then cut a long strip from a paper towel. The strip should be about an inch wide.
3. Using one of the felt-tip pens, make a mark across the paper towel about two inches from one end.
4. Place the strip on the rim of the glass with the inked end in the water. As the water wets the strip, notice the

colors that appear above the black ink.

5. Remove the paper towel strip and let it dry. Label the strip with the brand name of the pen.

6. Repeat the procedure for each different brand felt-tip pen. Notice the different pattern of colors each pen produces.

Now you can use these ink patterns to identify different felt-tip pens. Give a friend or family member a clean paper towel strip and your collection of black pens. Have the person make a mark across the strip with one of the pens. Make sure she or he does not tell you which pen was used. Then put the strip in a glass of water and compare its color pattern to the strips you already made. When you find the strip with the same color pattern, you can identify the pen.

STRESS

Checking Yourself

You can check your body for the signs of stress the next time you feel nervous before a test, sports event, speech, or some other special event.

1. You will need a watch or clock with a minute hand.

2. Check your heartbeat. Your pulse shows the rate of your heartbeat. Find your pulse by pressing your index and middle fingers against the inside of your wrist. Count the number of pulses you feel in one minute. When you are under stress, your heart will probably beat faster than usual. It might also feel like it is "pounding" in your chest.

3. Check your breathing. Notice how quickly and
   deeply you breathe. When you are under stress,
   you will probably breathe faster and your breaths
   will be shallower.
4. Check your perspiration. Examine the palms of
   your hands. Are they damp? When you are under
   stress, you will probably perspire more and your
   hands will get sweaty. You may also feel sweaty
   around your ears and neck.

Sometime when you are not feeling nervous, check
your heartbeat, breathing, and perspiration. Write
down your pulse and what you notice about your
breathing and perspiration. Then the next time you
feel nervous, you can use your notes to see how your
body changes under stress.

Glossary

amnesia the sudden loss of memory caused either by injury to the brain or by shock

appeal to ask to have a case considered again in a higher court

arsenic a white chemical powder that is very poisonous; arsenic is often used to kill rats, mice, and insects

bail the money offered to free an arrested person until a trial is held

burglary the breaking into a home or other building in order to steal something

chromatography a chemical process that separates out the substances that make up a mixture

comparison microscope a microscope that allows the user to view two objects at the same time

cross-examine to question a witness closely to check the truth of what she or he is saying

defendant a person accused of a crime in court

DNA a tiny particle in every cell of the body that determines a person's characteristics; all the cells in one person have the exact same DNA, but no two people (except identical twins) have exactly the same DNA

dusting powder a fine powder sprinkled on objects to reveal invisible fingerprints

evidence anything that can prove the guilt or innocence of a suspect in a criminal trial

eyewitness a person who actually sees a crime happening and can give a report of it

fingerprint the mark left on a surface by the unique pattern of ridges on a person's fingertip

forensic science the science that examines and studies evidence in criminal cases

gas chromatography a chemical process that turns a sample mixture into a gas, which then produces a pattern showing what the sample is made of

homicide the killing of one person by another person; murder

hypothesis a theory based on observed facts and used to explain evidence; once a hypothesis is made, it can be tested against other facts

microscope an instrument that greatly magnifies objects so details not visible to the naked eye can be seen

physical evidence the items gathered at a crime scene, such as paint, hair, fibers, fingerprints, footprints, tire tracks, wire, glass, papers, and weapons

polarized light microscope a microscope that allows the user to study the characteristics of materials such as fibers and crystals

polygraph an instrument that measures changes in a person's blood pressure, breathing, heartbeat, and perspiration while being questioned; also called a lie detector

prosecutor a lawyer who presents the case against a suspected criminal at a trial

robbery the stealing from a person by using force or threats; theft

solubility test a test to compare two or more samples by dipping them in different chemicals and observing how they react

stress the pressure or strain a person feels in upsetting or frightening situations

toxicology the science that studies poisons and their effects

voiceprint the pattern of sound waves created when a person speaks; no two people make exactly the same pattern

witness a person who has information that relates to a crime

Learn More About It

Here are some books to read to learn more about using science to solve crimes.

Adams, Barbara Johnston. *Crime Mysteries*. New York: Franklin Watts, 1988.

Barber, Jacqueline. *Crime Lab Chemistry*. Berkeley: Lawrence Science, 1989.

Bender, Lionel. *Forensic Detection*. New York: Gloucester Press, 1990.

Berger, Melvin. *Police Lab: Scientists at Work*. New York: John Day, 1976.

Blassingame, Wyatt. *Science Catches the Criminal*. New York: Dodd, Mead, 1975.

Block, Eugene B. *Lie Detectors: Their History and Use*. New York: David McKay, 1977.

Cobb, Vicki. *Chemically Active! Experiments You Can Do at Home*. New York: HarperCollins, 1985.

Cummings, Richard. *Be Your Own Detective: How to Conduct Investigations and Make Basic Equipment*. New York: David McKay, 1980.

Dautrich, Jack and Vivian Huff. *Big City Detective.* New York: Lodestar, 1986.

Gardner, Robert. *Crime Lab 101: Experimenting With Crime Detection.* New York: Walker, 1992.

Larranaga, Robert D. *Famous Crimefighters.* Minneapolis: Lerner Publications, 1970.

Millimaki, Robert H. *Fingerprint Detective.* Philadelphia: Lippincott, 1973.

Tesar, Jenny. *Scientific Crime Investigation.* New York: Franklin Watts, 1991.

Waters, John F. *Crime Labs: The Science of Forensic Medicine.* New York: Franklin Watts, 1979.

Zonderman, Jon. *Beyond the Crime Lab: The New Science of Investigation.* New York: John Wiley, 1990.

Index

IMPORTANT DATES IN CRIME INVESTIGATION

Principle behind the modern microscope was discovered by Zacharias Janssen of Holland. — 1590

1670s — **First simple microscope with powerful lenses was made by Anton van Leeuwenhoek of Holland.**

World's first detective agency was set up in France by Eugène François Vidocq. — 1810

1814 — **First scientific paper on detecting poisons was published by Mathieu Orfila of France.**

Principles for a reliable, professional police force were established by Robert Peel of England. — 1829

1836 — **Method for detecting tiny amounts of the poison arsenic was developed by James Marsh of England.**

First daytime police force in the United States was set up in Boston. — 1838

1850 — **First private detective agency in the United States was set up by Allan Pinkerton.**

System of identifying people by special body measurements was developed by Alphonse Bertillon of France. — 1879

1880s — **Sherlock Holmes detective stories, which used crime-solving methods based on science, were published.**

First hand-held camera was invented by George Eastman of the United States. — 1888

1892 — **Scientific system of classifying fingerprints was developed by Francis Galton of England.**

Idea of fingerprinting was made famous in a Mark Twain story about a country lawyer. — 1894